BESIDE STILL WATERS

Beside Still Waters

Guidance for Living from Psalm 23

by
David A. Palmer

2019

Some scripture quotations from The Authorized (King James) Version. Rights in the Authorized Version in the United Kingdom are vested in the Crown. Reproduced by permission of the Crown's patentee, Cambridge University Press

Some scripture quotations are from the New Revised Standard Version Bible, copyright © 1989 the Division of Christian Education of the National Council of the Churches of Christ in the United States of America. Used by permission. All rights reserved.

Copyright © 2019 by Dr. David A. Palmer

All rights reserved. This book or any portion thereof may not be reproduced or used in any manner whatsoever without the express written permission of the publisher except for the use of brief quotations in a book review or scholarly journal.

Printed in the United States of America

First Printing, 2019

ISBN 978-1-7321245-4-7

Place to Grow Press
1435 East Main Street
Kent, OH 44240

www.KentMethodist.org

Contents

Preface	vii
A Psalm of David	1
The Lord Is My Shepherd	3
No Wants	9
Green Pastures	13
Still Waters	19
He Restores My Soul	23
The Right Paths	27
For Whose Sake?	33
No Fear	37
Finding Comfort in Uncomfortable Times	43
God's Abundant Table	49
The Anointing	57
The Overflowing Cup	61
Surely Goodness and Mercy Shall Follow Me	65
I Will Dwell in the House of the Lord Forever	71
Notes	77

Preface

Of all the chapters in the sixty-six books of the Bible, a favorite for many people is Psalm 23. It is just 57 words in the original Hebrew; yet its words are so beautiful and compelling that they resonate deeply in the soul. In church practice, the Psalm is especially used at funerals; but its verses speak powerfully to many aspects of contemporary living. This book provides a journey through the twenty-third Psalm, and what it continues to say to people in the twenty-first century.

*The Lord is my shepherd; I shall not want.
He maketh me to lie down in green pastures:
he leadeth me beside the still waters.
He restoreth my soul: he leadeth me in the paths of
righteousness for his name's sake.
Yea, though I walk through the valley of the shadow of
death, I will fear no evil: for thou art with me;
thy rod and thy staff they comfort me.
Thou preparest a table before me in the presence of mine
enemies: thou anointest my head with oil;
my cup runneth over.
Surely goodness and mercy shall follow me all the days of
my life: and I will dwell in the house of the Lord for ever.*

Psalm 23 (KJV)

A Psalm of David

In the Hebrew Scriptures, the Psalm begins with the words, מִזְמוֹר לְדָוִד *mizmor l'David* – "A Psalm of David." Not all of the Psalms were written by David. Out of 150 Psalms, 73 are directly attributed to David; but even so, not all of those were necessarily written by David. A Psalm could be *dedicated to David* and given the heading, מִזְמוֹר לְדָוִד, because, although this is generally translated "a psalm *of* David," it could also mean "a psalm *to* David" or "*for* David." A few Psalms with this heading contain historical references later than David and thus are assuredly in the category of a psalm "dedicated to David."

Yet there is no reason to doubt that Psalm 23 is one of a number of psalms that were in fact written *by* David. Early Biblical passages identify David as a singer of songs who played the lyre (I Samuel 16), and on multiple occasions he led the people of Israel in worshipping with poetic song (see II Samuel 1 and I Chronicles 16). The psalms were typically songs used in worship, and it is completely consistent with David's skill and character that he would have written some of them. Psalm 23 is especially identifiable as a psalm written *by* David, because every verse of this psalm relates directly to David's life.

When David is first introduced in the Biblical story, he is a young boy, concerning whom his father Jesse says to the prophet Samuel, "He is out keeping the sheep." (I Samuel 16:11) Psalm 23 is sometimes called "a shepherd's psalm," because it draws so extensively on the imagery of shepherding in the ancient near east. David clearly was utilizing his childhood experiences with the flock in composing the psalm. Yet while the psalm builds on David's early life, it is believed that David actually wrote the psalm much later in his life, during one of his most difficult periods – the rebellion of Absalom. The story of David's son Absalom – his murder of his half-brother Amnon (in vengeance for Amnon's rape of Absalom's sister Tamar), his avoidance of any real discipline from his father, his suspicion (rightly) that the kingdom would go to someone else, his secret plot against his father, and finally his full-scale rebellion against David – can be found in II Samuel chapters 13 through 19. There are multiple points in Psalm 23 that relate to David's experience during this rebellion, and these will be noted in the chapters to follow. What is significant is that Psalm 23, as pleasant as it may seem in its initial verses, actually arose out of a time of great distress.

This is something of what gives the psalm its power. Psalm 23 is not a nice little poem written by someone sitting off in an ivory tower. It is the testimony of someone who faced enormous trouble, who at the same time was very painfully aware of his own flaws and failings, and who – in the midst of it all – found the answer in God. So the Psalm speaks in every age to people who are wrestling with life and faith, and who likewise can find the answer by trusting in the Lord, their Shepherd.

The Lord Is My Shepherd

The Lord is my shepherd...
Psalm 23:1a

The beginning of the psalm is so familiar that the contemporary reader is not struck with how bold an image this is for God. Outside of an obscure reference in a blessing of Jacob, this is the earliest place in the Bible where God is prominently pictured as a shepherd. David wrote this around 1000 BC. At that time in the ancient world, the popular image for a divine figure was that of a warrior. The gods were those mighty powers who would crush one's enemies. The idea that God is like a shepherd was a revolutionary picture for God, suggesting that God is near, gentle, and compassionate, ready to help the individual in need.

After Psalm 23, the image of God as shepherd would reappear at many points in the Bible. The prophet Isaiah would write, "The Lord will feed His flock like a shepherd; He will gather the lambs in His arms" (Isaiah 40:11); and the prophet Jeremiah would say, "The Lord will keep His people as a shepherd keeps the flock." (Jeremiah 30:10) The prophet Ezekiel, writing a half millennium after David, put forth the most extensive Old Testament image of God as shepherd in Ezekiel chapter 34.

Today people often find it pleasant to think of God as our shepherd. On the other hand, there is also something challenging about this image. If God is our shepherd, what does that make us? Sheep! Quite honestly, we are not inclined to think of ourselves as sheep. Sheep are dumb, they are stubborn, they are easily frightened, they run in herds, they get lost, and they are dependent and often helpless. If you ask people to pick an animal that they would like to have as a symbol for themselves, such as for a team mascot, they will likely pick something like a lion or a bear or a tiger or an eagle. We want to be in charge and powerful! In fact, the lion and the bear and the tiger and the eagle are all actual team mascots for numerous teams, and they are all national symbols of various countries. But there are no sports teams that want to be sheep, with the exception of a few teams who have a ram for a mascot, which is normally a bighorn sheep, where the ram is a formidable figure. Ordinary sheep don't make the grade.

But if we are truly honest with ourselves, we likely discover that there are some real parallels between sheep and our human condition. As human beings, we are often stubborn. We are easily frightened. We run in herds. We lose our way. We get in trouble. As Isaiah put it, "All we like sheep have gone astray." (Isaiah 53:6) To recognize that we are like sheep and that God is our Shepherd is to come finally to a key spiritual insight: we need God. We are not self-sufficient and all-powerful. We need a Shepherd.

In this context, it is quite striking that David, of all people, acclaimed God as his shepherd. David was the greatest king in the history of Israel. He defeated one foe after another and pushed the borders of his country to their greatest extent. If he looked at the great kings in the world around him, he could easily have defined *himself* as the "shepherd" for his people. Hammurabi, the glorious king of ancient Babylon, had famously said of himself, "I am the shepherd of the people, who causes the truth to appear, guiding my flock rightly."[i] David could easily have fallen under the illusion that he was self-sufficient and all-powerful, the source of guidance and hope for his people. But at the outset of Psalm 23, David recognized that he himself was not the shepherd. The Lord is the shepherd. David recognized his fundamental need for God.

It is to this kind of self-awareness that the psalm at its outset urges every reader. In the sheep image, the psalm makes plain that we are limited creatures who on our own will be lost. But the psalm proclaims that we have a Shepherd, and with that image, the psalm lifts up several key truths about God.

What does a shepherd do for sheep? A shepherd, first of all, *cares* for the sheep. A good shepherd is concerned for the well-being of each sheep, and works to see that the sheep have their needs met. This caring aspect of the shepherd is accented by the prophet Isaiah, when he says that God as shepherd "will feed his flock" and "will gather the lambs in his arms." (Isaiah 40:11) A shepherd also provides *guidance* for the sheep, leading them in the right paths to good pastures and watering places, images that will come forth in later verses in the psalm. Furthermore, a shepherd provides *protection* for the sheep, defending them against predators and dangers of all sorts. To say that God is our shepherd is to say that there can be a very close and sustaining relationship between ourselves and God, in which we know God's care, guidance, and protection in our daily life. God is not some distant deity; but God is near, to be actively engaged with us – just as a shepherd is close to the sheep.

There is at this point another key element that is quite notable in the first phrase of the twenty-third Psalm. David does not simply say, "The Lord is a shepherd." He says, "The Lord is *my* shepherd." He affirms a direct personal connection with God. The psalm invites everyone to this kind of intimate personal relationship with

God – where God is not simply a theoretical concept, but where God becomes *our* shepherd.

At the same time, the twenty-third Psalm does not encourage *private* religion. Today there are many people who want to think that they do not need any connection with a faith community. They can just have their own private thing with God. But while Biblical faith is personal, it is not private. Consider again the shepherd image. How many shepherds have one sheep? Shepherds have flocks of sheep! The whole image of the shepherd creates the sense that God is leading people not in a solitary spiritual venture but in company with others. This in fact is a principle that is evident throughout the Bible. Whether one looks at the people of Israel in the Old Testament or the twelve disciples following Jesus or the early church, it is clear that people grow in a relationship with God as they share in a *community* of faith with one another. This is why God draws people into connection with the church today! If we want to share in the kind of experience that David describes in the twenty-third Psalm, we need not only to be led by the shepherd but to be joined with the shepherd's flock.

The image of God as shepherd continues throughout the Old Testament and comes finally to a fulfillment in the New Testament in Jesus, who said "I am the good shepherd." (John 10:11) Later the book of Hebrews would refer to Jesus as "the great shepherd of the sheep." (Hebrews 13:20) Just as the image of shepherd in the Old Testament becomes a central image for God, so this image will come to encapsulate who Jesus is – one who watches over us, who seeks after us, who calls us to come to him, and who is so committed to human beings that he offers his life for us; as Jesus said, "I lay down my life for the sheep." (John 10:15) In Jesus, the extraordinary insight of Psalm 23, that the Lord is like a *shepherd*, comes to its climax – in the One whose love and devotion to us is without limit.

No Wants

> *I shall not want.*
> **Psalm 23:1b**

The first verse of Psalm 23 concludes with the statement, "I shall not want." What a statement for the present age! People want all the time. Contemporary society is geared toward enticing people to want more and more. When Psalm 23 speaks of "not wanting," it directly contradicts the consumerism and endless grasping of today's world.

Yet it seems too much to say that one ought simply to want nothing, since people may desire some goals that are very good and right. The Bible speaks of "longing for God" (Isaiah 26:9) or desiring God—a worthy desire indeed! So what exactly is Psalm 23 saying?

The meaning of the Psalm becomes clear when we understand that the original Hebrew in verse one—לֹא אֶחְסָר (*lo echsar*)—is most precisely translated, "I shall not lack." In other words, it means "I shall not be *in want*" or "I shall lack nothing." The full meaning of "The Lord is my Shepherd; I shall not want" is that when we trust in God, we can be freed both from grasping and from worry, because we know we will have all that we need.

Does this mean that believers will never lack for good health or good fortune or pleasant circumstances? That cannot be what this means, because of the experiences of David himself. When David wrote Psalm 23—in the latter part of his life—he had already had numerous experiences of loss and privation. There was a time when, as a young man, he had to flee for his life from King Saul, and he was lacking a great deal. As a parent, he suffered the deaths of several of his children. One of his darkest moments came when his son, Absalom, rebelled against his throne; and it is precisely during this extremely low point in David's life that scholars believe he wrote Psalm 23.

The rebellion began when Absalom secretly raised a rebel army and then advanced upon Jerusalem to seize the throne from his father. David, hearing of the rebellion, fled from Jerusalem in great haste with a small company of followers. Full of grief, he made his way to the distant small city of Mahanaim, located far across the Jordan, about one hundred miles from Jerusalem. There, it is believed, he wrote the psalm. That would mean that Psalm 23 was written when David had lost or was on the verge of losing just about everything—his family, his home, his kingship, and his life. How could he possibly say, "The Lord is my shepherd, I lack nothing"?

What David had found, through all his trials, was that no matter what on this earth he may lack, if he had God, he had what he needed.

One day in a Sunday School class, a little girl stood up to recite the twenty-third Psalm. She began, "The Lord is my shepherd, He's all I want." Surely she got it right! Psalm 23 declares that God is the answer to what we need. It encourages us *to want above all a relationship with God;* because when we come into the care of the Shepherd, we find that God will sustain us even in the midst of great trials, God will amply provide, and we will find our true satisfaction not finally in passing things but in the sure blessings of God.

The basic human problem is not that people have wants or desires, but that they direct their desires in the wrong way. This was a lesson that David had learned earlier in his life, especially through painful experience.

There was a time, when he was younger, when David was not yet at the spiritual level reflected in Psalm 23, that he got carried away with what he thought he wanted. He was king in Jerusalem, highly successful, living in great wealth and power, having a large family, adored by his subjects; he seemed to have everything. But he wanted more. His eye fell on a woman next door, Bathsheba, and he began an adulterous relationship that nearly ruined everything. When he was finally confronted by the prophet Nathan, he was forced to recognize that he had gotten grievously off track. He acknowledged his sin; and he repented—which means not only that he felt deeply sorry for his sin, but he turned his life around. He directed his life afresh toward God. He realized that it was only through faith in God that he would find what he truly needed.

People today so often think that they need something more—a better job, a better house, a better car. Maybe you do need a better car... but Psalm 23 says that what you really need is God. When we take hold of the Lord as our shepherd, then we are on the path toward a truly blessed life. This is why Jesus said, "Seek first the Kingdom of God, and then all else will be added unto you." (Matthew 6:33)

In a world in which people are grasping after much, yet find real satisfaction in little, Psalm 23 directs us to the Source of real wholeness in life. The answer is to lift our heart to the Lord our Shepherd and find in God's presence that we are no longer in want.

Green Pastures

He maketh me to lie down in green pastures.
Psalm 23:2a

One of the challenges in truly understanding Psalm 23 is that it is full of shepherding images; and most contemporary people know very little about shepherding, especially as it is practiced in the Middle East. For example, David speaks of green pastures, which are common in many parts of America. Yet in the dry climate of Israel, pastures are often not green! They are brown much of the time; and thus the image of green pastures is an image of great abundance. Another image that David puts forth is that of sheep lying down. The reality is that sheep are normally standing. The image of sheep lying down in the pasture is thus a very special image of rest and peace.

A particularly enlightening book in this regard, which has become something of a classic, is one entitled *A Shepherd Looks at Psalm 23*. The author, Phillip Keller, had years of experience as an actual shepherd, running ranching operations in various places, and he viewed the twenty-third Psalm from that perspective. Keller noted that in order for sheep to lie down in a pasture, four things are necessary.

The sheep must have freedom from fear. They are not about to lie down if they think that a wolf might be just over the rise.

The sheep must have freedom from friction with one another. Sheep in a flock, it seems, are constantly battling for position; they have what shepherds call a "butting order." They regularly butt heads or intimidate one another, and as long as they are concerned about fighting for position against another sheep they will not lie down.

The sheep must also have freedom from pests. Flies and other bugs bother sheep a lot, and they cannot lie down if they are constantly shaking off pests.

Finally, sheep must have a full belly.

Sheep don't lie down very much.

You may note that there are strong parallels between the things that agitate sheep and the things that agitate us. We are troubled by fear, especially fears about potentially serious threats. We are troubled by friction with other people. We are troubled by all sorts of irritating things that "bug" us. And we get worried about not having enough. So we may find that we don't lie down very much either, in a spiritual sense and maybe even in a physical sense; it can be hard for us to come to a state of peace.

In working with sheep, Phillip Keller noted that what calms sheep the most is the presence of the shepherd.[ii] This of course is the central message of Psalm 23 – that when we have the Lord as our Shepherd, we have the fundamental answer to all those troubles which would rob us of peace.

We have the answer, first of all, to fear. When the shepherd appears among a flock of sheep, the sheep become noticeably more relaxed, primarily because they see the shepherd as a protector – the wolves are at bay as long as the shepherd is at hand. This is what happens in the Biblical story when people become aware that God is among them – they are able to find release from fear. Consider, for example, how the Christmas story unfolds when scribes recall how the prophets had said, "From you, Bethlehem, shall come a ruler who is to shepherd my people Israel." (Matt 2: 6) When that divine shepherd appears in Bethlehem, angels announce his birth by saying, "Fear not." (Luke 2:10) They say that to a group of shepherds among their sheep, so that we get the point that when the Lord our Shepherd is among us, we no longer need to be afraid; or as Zechariah, the father of John the Baptist, proclaimed of the Messiah, "Being rescued from the hands of our enemies, we might serve the Lord without fear." (Luke 1:73)

Of course, the wolves are still out there. There are terrible evils in the news every day, and you may be confronted by all kinds of threats in your own life. But what David understood is that the shepherd is stronger than the wolves. The twenty-third Psalm is telling us that we need not fear when we put our trust in God.

The shepherd can also bring freedom from friction with our neighbors. How often do we get agitated by other people? Today there seems to be ever more conflict in the society at large. Especially in the realm of politics, people are feeling increasing animosity toward those on the "other side." But concerning his flocks of sheep, Philip Keller reported that "whenever I came into view and my presence attracted their attention, the sheep quickly forgot their foolish rivalries and stopped their fighting."[iii] How much do we need the divine Shepherd's presence among us today, to move us past divisions and bickering, so that we might work in positive ways together! Instead of constantly butting heads with each other, we are drawn by the Lord our shepherd into a spiritual unity, in the harmony of the Lord's flock.

The shepherd in the field also brings relief from all those bugs that pester sheep. Even in ancient times, shepherds applied ointments to sheep that acted as bug repellents, and modern shepherds have various sprays to drive off those pests. Today there are all sorts of irritations that can disturb us—whether it is physical ailments or annoying problems in life or just the things that go wrong in the course of any day. It is hard to be at peace when there are constantly irritants that annoy us. But when the Lord our shepherd is near, God's Spirit can function in us like a soothing balm. As the Psalmist said in Psalm 94, "When cares increase in my heart, Your consolation calms my soul." (Psalm 94:19)

Finally, the shepherd answers the sheep's yearning for a full belly by leading the sheep to the best pasture. Likewise, the Lord our Shepherd would satisfy our deepest needs, and this is especially what is symbolized in the image of sheep lying down in green pasture. There is a fascinating story along this line in the gospel of Mark about Jesus feeding the 5000. Mark reports that Jesus encountered a large group of people, and He saw that "they were like sheep without a shepherd." (Mark 6:34) Jesus began to teach them. It started to get late, and the people did not have any food. So Jesus, Mark says, had the people "sit down in groups on the green grass." (Mark 6:39) Mark specifically says *green* grass for a reason—because he sees Jesus here enacting the twenty-third Psalm. He makes his flock lie down in green pastures; and he feeds the five thousand so that "all ate and were filled." (Mark 6:42) The clear message of the story is that Jesus, the Good Shepherd, will abundantly provide for his people, not only physically but spiritually. Christ satisfies what we truly need.

Five hundred years after David wrote the twenty-third Psalm, the prophet Ezekiel proclaimed, "Thus says the Lord God: I myself will search for my sheep, and will seek them out.... I will feed them with good pasture, on the mountain heights of Israel; there they shall lie down in good grazing land, and they shall feed on rich pasture on the mountains of Israel. I myself will be the shepherd of my sheep, and I will make them lie down, says the Lord God." (Ezekiel 34:11–15) Clearly, Ezekiel was saying that God in a decisive way would carry out the themes of the twenty-third Psalm; and that prophecy would come to its ultimate fulfillment five hundred years later in Jesus. Jesus appears among us as One who seeks the lost. He is the Good Shepherd, who provides for our deepest needs and enables us finally to "lie down in green pastures."

Still Waters

He leadeth me beside the still waters
Psalm 23:2b

The image of still waters is very peaceful, and intentionally so in this psalm, because the Hebrew word translated as "still" – מְנֻחוֹת *menuchot* – has the basic meaning of "restful." You have very likely been on vacation someplace, or on some sort of outing, where you were "beside still waters," and felt a sense of peace. But what is striking about Psalm 23 is that these words were not written by David when he was on vacation at some peaceful spot. He wrote this when he was in one of the most stressful circumstances in his life – during the rebellion of Absalom! Imagine how David felt when his own son seized the capital city of Jerusalem, and David was running for his life. Huddled for refuge in the remote town of Mahanaim, David composed Psalm 23 – when he was in grief over the faithlessness of his son, when the outcome of the rebellion was completely uncertain, and when it might all end for David not only with the loss of his kingdom but the loss of his life. How, in such circumstances, could he talk about God leading him beside still waters? It was an extraordinary statement, which declares that God can bring peace even in the midst of the most turbulent times.

Shepherds know that when it comes to drinking water, sheep very much prefer still waters. They do not like rushing streams at all, because the turbulent water makes them fear that they might be swept away. For centuries, shepherds in the Middle East, if they needed to water their sheep at a fast-flowing stream, have responded to that situation by putting rocks or sod in the water to make a little dam that would create a quiet pool along the edge of the stream. Perhaps David had this practice in mind when he spoke of God leading to still waters. If so, then the image would suggest that even if the waters of life are turbulent, God can still the waters. Indeed the Hebrew translated "still waters" could also be translated "stilled waters"–rough waters that have been quieted. This would connect with one of the most memorable stories of Jesus, when he was with the disciples in a boat during a storm on the Sea of Galilee, and he commanded the waves, saying, "Peace, be still!" At that moment, the Scripture says, "the wind ceased, and there was a complete calm." (Mark 4:39) The message, both in that gospel story and in Psalm 23, is that the life of faith may not always be smooth, but even in the midst of very stressful times, one can find in the Lord a profound peace.

There is another aspect of David's past that might be reflected in the image of still waters. When he was a young adult, David became a successful general fighting to free the Israelites from Philistine oppression. King Saul, however, became jealous of David's success, fearing that David might become a threat, and he began to seek David's life. David was forced to flee from Saul into the wilderness, and he came into the region around the Dead Sea. The Dead Sea valley is one of the most desolate areas on earth. There is a large body of water, of course; but the Dead Sea has so much salt you cannot even sink in it. Nothing lives there, and of course you cannot drink the water. But in that bleak environment David came to Ein Gedi, an oasis that is near the Dead Sea. It is a wonderfully lush and peaceful spot. Freshwater springs create waterfalls and pools, supporting abundant greenery and animal life. There David found a refuge. Perhaps he had that experience in the back of his mind when he wrote of God, "He leadeth me beside the still waters." The meaning again is that even in the most difficult times, we can find, through faith in God, a place of refreshment and renewal.

In the fall of 2018, Hurricane Florence brought devastation to the Carolinas, with sustained winds and an unrelenting rainfall that brought extensive flooding. The danger of the hurricane was broadly announced in advance of its landfall, and many people boarded up their homes and businesses and evacuated the area. In Myrtle Beach, there was a coffee shop where the windows had been boarded up with plywood; and one board had words boldly written upon it proclaiming, "God is good." How could someone say, "God is good," when a huge hurricane was coming, forcing evacuation, making the coffee shop close its doors, and threatening major destruction?

The person who wrote that sign could do so for the same reason that David, in desperate circumstances at Mahanaim, could say that the Lord leads us by still waters. It is because even in the midst of a storm, we can find strength and peace and life when we trust in God. On the sign at that coffee shop, there was also a reference to Psalm 91, verses one through sixteen. Those verses were not the source of the statement, "God is good," which is found instead in other psalms. The person who wrote on that board clearly intended that people should look at Psalm 91, which says:

"You who live in the shelter of the Most High, who abide in the shadow of the Almighty, will say to the Lord, 'My refuge and my fortress; my God, in whom I trust.' You will not fear the terror of the night ... or the destruction that wastes at noonday ... because you have made the Lord your refuge, the Most High your dwelling place... 'When they call to me,' says the Lord, 'I will answer them; I will be with them in trouble, I will rescue them and honor them. With long life I will satisfy them, and show them my salvation.'" (from Psalm 91:1–16)

This is the core message of Psalm 23 – that we find sure help and protection in the presence of God. There is much in this world that would cause us distress, but we can arrive at still waters as we put our trust in the Divine Shepherd.

He Restores My Soul

He restoreth my soul.
                                        Psalm 23:3a

Many contemporary people, when they think of the word "soul," imagine some purely spiritual part of the self that floats off to heaven after death. But ancient Hebrews had a much more holistic view of the human being. They realized that we are a complex blend of physical and spiritual aspects that form the whole living self. They had a word, *nephesh,* which denoted that entire self; and it is this word that appears in Psalm 23 verse two, in the phrase that is traditionally translated "my soul" – נַפְשִׁי. Because *nephesh* refers to the totality of the physical, emotional, cognitive, and spiritual aspects of a sentient being, the word can be used to refer to higher animals (such as dogs, cats, or sheep) as well as to human beings. The phrase "he restoreth my soul" is thus not referring to some otherworldly transaction; it speaks of the power of the Shepherd to bring restoration to a living being who is in some kind of trouble.

    The phrase is therefore directly applicable to the situation of sheep. It is significant that the Hebrew phrase translated "he restores" – יְשׁוֹבֵב (*yishovev*) – has the sense of "he brings back." This relates to a key problem in the life of sheep, the problem of getting lost.

    You likely recall that favorite nursery rhyme that has to do with shepherding – about Little Bo Peep. "Little Bo

Peep has lost her sheep and can't tell where to find them. Leave them alone, and they'll come home, bringing their tails behind them." This little rhyme is never used as a manual for shepherds, first of all because Little Bo Peep was obviously not very good at shepherding! She lost apparently not just one of her sheep but all of them. But more than that, the advice given in this nursery rhyme is all wrong! Leave sheep alone and they won't come home. Sheep have a terrible sense of direction and are in serious trouble when they get lost.[iv] This is why a key role of a shepherd is to retrieve lost sheep.

A fundamental problem in human life is that people lose their way. We wander off from God, and can find ourselves in serious trouble. Psalm 23 is telling us that the Lord our shepherd is at work to bring us back, to restore us to life with God. The prophet Ezekiel, who built extensively on the imagery of Psalm 23, reiterated that theme as he declared:

"My sheep were scattered, they wandered all over the mountains, with no one to search for them. But thus says the Lord God, 'I myself will search for my sheep. I will rescue them from all the places to which they have been scattered.... I will seek the lost and bring back the strays, I will bind up the injured and strengthen the weak.'" (Ezekiel 14:6,11–12,16)

Jesus carried that theme yet further in his parable of the lost sheep. As he said, "Which one of you, having a hundred sheep and losing one of them, does not leave the ninety-nine in the wilderness and go after the one that is lost until he finds it? When he has found it, he lays it on his shoulders and rejoices. And when he comes home, he calls together his friends and neighbors, saying to them, 'Rejoice with me, for I have found my sheep that was lost.'" (Luke 15:4–6)

In this parable, Jesus builds upon the broad awareness among people in his day that a shepherd, having lost a sheep, will surely go searching diligently after it, and will rejoice when the sheep is found. This illuminates what we are to understand when the Scripture says that the Lord is our shepherd. God is not passively waiting for us to somehow find our way to God. God searches for us. As Ezekiel said of God, "I myself will search for my sheep… I will seek after the lost and bring back the strays." If we become aware of God, it is because God has come to us.

The saving act of the shepherd is finally to bring the sheep back out of trouble. This is a picture of what God does for all humanity through Jesus Christ. God reaches to us through Christ, to bring us back, out of our condition of spiritual lostness, into life and fellowship with God.

The restoration of which Psalm 23 speaks is primarily a restoring of the individual to spiritual life. "He restoreth my soul." Yet the theme of restoration also has broader implications. When a lost sheep is brought back, it is not only brought back into the care of the shepherd, but it is brought back to the flock. The restoration for which the shepherd works is also a restoration of community.

Ezekiel spoke strongly along this line about the work of God the Shepherd to bring wholeness to a broken community. Ezekiel viewed with disgust the way that some people in his day were exploiting other people and wrecking the fabric of life for others. Using the imagery of the flock, he said, "Is it not enough for you to feed on the good pasture, but you must tread down with your feet the rest of the pasture? When you drink of clear water, must you foul the rest with your feet? Therefore, thus says the Lord God: I myself will judge between the fat sheep and the lean sheep. Because you pushed with flank and shoulder, and butted at all the weak animals with your horns until you scattered them far and wide, I will save my flock, and they shall no longer be ravaged; and I will judge between sheep and sheep. I will set up over them one shepherd, my servant David, and he shall feed them: he shall feed them and be their shepherd." (Ezekiel 34:18–23) So Ezekiel spoke of how God would intercede on behalf of the disenfranchised and the weak, and how God finally would "set up one shepherd, my servant David." This refers not to David himself, who had died five hundred years earlier, but to the descendant of David, namely, the Messiah.

The Good Shepherd is thus at work to bring wholeness, not only to the individual lost soul, but to the entire society. As always, the message of the twenty-third Psalm is deeply personal, but it is not private; because those who experience the redemptive power of the Shepherd will be joined with the Shepherd's work to bring well-being and peace to all.

The Right Paths

He leadeth me in the paths of righteousness
Psalm 23:3b

Psalm 23 is one of the few sections of Scripture that are still commonly quoted in the King James Version. There are three good reasons for this. First, the Psalm has such a deep-seated traditional use in the church—especially at funerals or times of personal trial—that there is real value in using a translation that has a long history and that is firmly rooted in the memory of many parishioners. Secondly, the King James Version has a beautiful poetic form, which captures something of the poetic rhythm of the Hebrew original. Finally, the particular wording used in the King James translation of Psalm 23 manages to capture some important nuances, which may be lost in some other translations. It is for these reasons that the King James Version of the psalm is used in this book.

At the same time, it can be valuable to consult modern translations of the psalm. There are, of course, a few English-speaking churches that want to insist that the King James Version is the *only* authoritative God-inspired translation; they will even advertise themselves as "KJV churches." But when the Bible says that "all Scripture is inspired by God" (II Timothy 3:16), it means that the Spirit of God was guiding the Biblical writers and editors, and they were writing in Hebrew and Greek, not King

James English! When it came to translating the Hebrew and Greek into English, the committee appointed by King James of England did do a very good job—in 1611. But scholars have made a good deal of progress in understanding Hebrew and Greek since then, and people don't talk like King James anymore; so the best way generally to read the Bible today is to use a good modern translation, of which there are several.

For Psalm 23, modern translations quite often render verse 3 as: "He leads/guides me in *right paths*." (New Revised Standard Version; New International Version) This is a good, accurate, and straightforward translation of the original Hebrew; and reading the verse this way helps to connect the psalm once again to the experience of sheep. One of the key problems that sheep face is that they get off track and can end up hopelessly lost. This can happen very easily in a semi-arid landscape such as that of Israel, where there are lots of openings through sparse brush, and various gullies, and old tracks that other animals have made. It is not uncommon that a sheep will wander onto a false path leading into desolate and dangerous country.

A central role of the shepherd is therefore, as the psalm says, "to lead in right paths." Throughout the Bible, God appears precisely in this role. There are times when God literally leads people, such as when God led the people of Israel out of Egypt through the wilderness. As the book of Exodus says, "The Lord went in front of them, in a pillar of cloud by a day and pillar of fire by night, to *lead* them along the way" (Exodus 13:21) More often, God leads people spiritually, guiding people to go in the right direction in life, to be able to live their life rightly. A good example is Psalm 143, as it offers a prayer to God for guidance: "Teach me, O Lord the way I should go... let your good Spirit *lead* me on a level path." (Psalm 143:8,10) In these passages and in Psalm 23:3, the word translated "lead" is the Hebrew word נָחָה *nachah*, which has a sense of guiding in a way of blessing.

The problem, however, is that human beings often do not pay attention to God's leading and stray off the right path. David did this in a disastrous way when he got into an adulterous relationship with Bathsheba. But when David was confronted by the prophet Nathan, he repented, and turned back to God. That experience of getting back onto the right track with God was very likely in David's mind when he wrote of God, "He leads me in right paths."

Still further, it is not only individuals who can get on the wrong path in life; whole societies can get off track. This occurred during the history of Israel when the people of Israel began increasingly to ignore God's leading. The prophets spoke very often along this line about how the people were on the wrong track; and they warned that this would result in disaster. The warnings came to fruition in the sixth century BC, as the people of Judah were conquered by the Babylonian empire and carried off into exile. The prophet Jeremiah, living in the midst of that period, spoke of how God had been seeking continually to lead the people in paths of blessing, but they had turned away. He said:

"Thus says the Lord: 'Stand at the crossroads, and look, and ask for the ancient paths, where the good way lies; and walk in it, and find rest for your souls.' But they said, 'We will not walk in it.' 'I raised up sentinels for you [likely referring to the many prophets of Israel]: "Give heed to the sound of the trumpet!"' But they said, 'We will not give heed.'" (Jeremiah 6:16–17) That refusal to give heed to God led finally to the trauma of the exile, when the people spent fifty years in bondage in Babylon. All this raises the question, of course, as to whether human beings are on the right path today.

"Ask where the good way lies," says Jeremiah, "and walk in in, and find rest for your souls." (Jeremiah 6:16) This image of getting on the right path appears repeatedly throughout the Bible. But what exactly is the right path, and how do you know when you are on it?

A common attitude today is that the right path is whatever feels right to you at the moment. But when sheep are wandering off toward disaster, the errant path onto which they are wandering is exactly what feels right to them at the moment! People need some sort of greater guidance to be and stay on the right path.

Here it is very helpful to recognize that in Psalm 23 the phrase that can be translated "right paths" also means "paths of righteousness." The King James Version is correct; and this is a case where the King James translation is lifting up an important nuance. The Hebrew word meaning "right" or "righteous" is the word צֶדֶק *tsedek*. It denotes that which is morally right and good, that which is just and upright. So *the right path is the righteous path*. The right path is the way that is in harmony with God's principles of goodness and justice.

Too often today, individuals or corporate entities or entire political alliances will choose to do simply whatever brings short-term profit or advantage. Psalm 23 calls human beings to a much higher ethic–to do what is genuinely right and good. The Psalm also makes clear how people can know what is truly right and good–by looking to the Lord, the divine Shepherd; for God is at work to guide people onto the right path, if they only pay heed. As the Psalmist said in Psalm 25, "Good and upright is the Lord... God leads the humble in what is right." (Psalm 25:8–9)

Nevertheless, there are times when, even if we want to be on the right path, we err and go off down the wrong way. The prophet Isaiah spoke about this universal human pattern of getting off track when he said, "All we like sheep have gone astray." (Isaiah 53:6) But it is highly significant that Isaiah goes on in that same passage to speak of how the Suffering Servant–Christ–would take upon himself all our sins, so that we can be forgiven and brought back onto the right path with God. There is no false path upon which we enter that is finally a "path of no return." The Lord our Shepherd is gracious; and when we are receptive to God, we can experience the Lord's mercy and be brought afresh onto the right path in life.

In the end, Psalm 23 moves us to seriously consider what path we are on. At times we may sense that we have drifted off track. At times we may feel like a sheep that is looking at multiple apparent paths, not sure which way to go. Wherever we are, the answer is to look to the Shepherd, who will meet us with grace, and lead us in those paths of righteousness wherein we share in the genuine goodness of the Lord.

For Whose Sake?

...for His name's sake.
Psalm 23:3c

If the right path is the righteous path, this means that those who journey with God will be actively involved in doing good in the world. But it is quite notable that after the phrase, "He leadeth me in the paths of righteousness," the psalm continues by saying, "for His name's sake." Here the psalm speaks of more than simply doing what is good; it addresses the fundamental question of what motivates people.

What is it that motivates people to do good today? To answer that, consider a simple and common scenario. Suppose that you are a high school administrator considering how to raise money for the sports boosters and the music boosters at the school. You could simply say to people, "Please contribute quietly to the booster fund, and we will keep everything you do a secret." Administrators know that this will not work. There are three basic approaches that do commonly work and that are broadly used.

First, appeal to people's vanity! People love recognition, so if you promise to put their name in the program or somewhere, they are more likely to give. Some people do not really care about that, of course; but there are plenty who do, and this is why institutions regularly use this technique on a grand scale. It especially works well if you can have many different giving levels that are also published, so that people can see that their neighbor or classmate is giving more, and then they feel compelled to move up to the next level so that they don't look cheap!

A second good technique is to appeal to people's greed. Offer the possibility of a big cash payout! Thus we have the popularity of raffles. People especially love charity raffles, because even if they lose, they can at least console themselves with the fact that they contributed to a good cause. In a 50/50, the cause, of course, only gets fifty percent of the funds put forward; but it is the promised potential of reward that motivates a lot of giving.

The third technique is the fundraiser – running concession stands, for example. This is more difficult, because it requires the existence of some genuinely goodhearted, hardworking people who will volunteer to staff the concession stands for no tangible benefit at all. But all that is needed is a relatively small group of such people. The funds are generated by the fact that lots of people will readily spend their money for snacks.

In each of these approaches, people contribute their funds to a cause in exchange for some reward. If I put forth my money, I can get my name in print, or I might win the raffle, or I at least get a hot dog! In each case, I am motivated to do some good, because it is, at least to some degree, for *my* sake. I am getting personal benefit or glory.

It would not be fair to fault school administrators or any institutions that use these techniques. They find that in today's world, these are the only sorts of techniques that work for their setting. In taking these approaches, they are in fact building upon a Biblical assessment of the human condition – that human beings are naturally self-centered. Techniques that entice people to give by offering rewards or recognitions are cleverly exploiting that natural self-centeredness, to produce some real good in the end. But such techniques only go so far. Total giving by non-churchgoing people in America, through every avenue, amounts to around 1% of their annual income.

If you go to most any church, you will find that the church does not use any of these techniques. When you put something into the church offering plate, your name does not go up onto a projection screen or appear later in a list of donors in the church newsletter, nor is there a moment at the end of worship when they draw an envelope number and announce the winner of the day's lottery. You will probably find that you can get a snack at church, if you go to the fellowship time that is offered, but that is free! The church does not offer any tangible rewards for doing good. Why not? It is because when we are following the Lord our Shepherd, we do good for His name's sake.

That simple phrase – "for His name's sake" – points to the heart of the spiritual transformation that Jesus would bring about in human life. It is the movement from the self-centered life to the God-centered life. Jesus spoke to this when he called people to "deny yourself to follow Christ" (Mark 8), and to "seek first the kingdom of God" (Matthew 6). The movement from self-centeredness toward God-centeredness is also behind Jesus' teaching about giving when he said, "Whenever you give, do not sound a trumpet before you... so as to be praised by others. But when you give, do not let your left hand know what your right hand is doing, so that your giving may be done in secret." (Matthew 6:2-4) The church is unique in society as an institution whose primary means of raising funds involves people quietly giving in secret. This works in the church because people are motivated to give, and to engage in service to others, out of a commitment to God. When people walk in paths of righteousness – doing good – for *His* name's sake, they are drawn beyond themselves into much larger purposes and a much higher calling, into the work of God's Kingdom; and the glory goes to God. This is why churches in America are the source of the great majority of charitable giving and service in society,[v] because people are on a path in which it is not, in the end, about self-gain or self-glorification but about God.

In sum, the "right paths" lead people not simply to experience personal blessing, but to become instruments of God's blessing for the world, because God's paths lead into a sharing in God's purposes of love for all.

No Fear

Yea, though I walk through the valley of the shadow of death, I will fear no evil, for thou art with me.
Psalm 23:4a

The image of walking through the valley of the shadow of death is perhaps the most gripping image in Psalm 23. Walking through a valley could be a pleasant experience, if it is a nice scenic valley! But this is a different sort of valley – the valley of the shadow of death. The Hebrew term that is translated here as "shadow of death" is a single Hebrew word: צַלְמָוֶת – *tsalmavet*. The word appears eighteen times in the Old Testament, where it always indicates a place of darkness and gloom, a place of great trouble and threat. At times it is used to denote the place of the dead. The valley of tsalmavet, the valley of the shadow of death, is a place you do not want to enter, but you might find yourself there anyways.

The image finds an immediate point of reference in David's experience with shepherding. In the rugged hill country of Israel there are numerous steep ravines. A sheep that ends up in one of those chasms can find itself hemmed in, often in the shadows, with no food or water, and perhaps no apparent way out; and who knows what predator might be around the next turn? The "valley of the shadow of death" could be a very literal place for a sheep.

But the valley of the shadow of death is also an image that connects very much with human life; and it certainly connected with several difficult experiences in David's life. There was the time when he stood in front of Goliath, or the time when he was fleeing from the murderous designs of King Saul; but David was in the deepest valley of this sort at the moment when he wrote the psalm. In the midst of the rebellion of Absalom, when the rebel army had the upper hand, David was squarely in the valley of the shadow of death.

The natural feeling in such a circumstance is fear. Today you may find yourself in a variety of circumstances that give serious reason for fear. A threat to your health, or a financial loss, or a conflict with someone, or a problem in your family are all anxiety-producing; or it may be circumstances in the larger society that produce fear – the division, the hatefulness, the violence, and the uncertainty of this age. In many ways, people find themselves journeying through the valley of the shadow of death – and experience a sense of dread.

Yet in Psalm 23 David says, "Though I walk through the valley of the shadow of death, I will fear no evil." (Psalm 23:4) He is in the dark valley but proclaims that he does not fear. This is not bravado. It is not a case of David imagining that he is just so tough, mustering up the spunk to proclaim, "I refuse to be afraid." Such bravado can look bold on the outside; but often when people loudly proclaim that they are not afraid, it is just a mask for the terror that they actually feel deep inside. David, however, had a solid reason to not fear. One can gain insight into that by looking back into David's past to the story of Goliath.

When Goliath strode onto the battlefield, he was a champion warrior, of the most outsized proportions, who had brutally slain many an opponent. He mockingly shouted to the young David, "Come to me, and I will give your flesh to the birds of the air and the beasts of the field." (I Samuel 17:44) No one else in Israel had been willing to go up against Goliath because they had all been absolutely terrified; and David appeared to have no chance. David responded to Goliath not with bravado but with faith. He replied, "You come to me with sword and spear and javelin, but I come to you in the name of the Lord . . . The battle is God's." (I Samuel 17:45,47) David did not fear because he trusted, with his whole heart, that God was with him.

Years later, facing an even larger giant in the rebel army of Absalom, David wrote, "Though I walk through the valley of the shadow of death, I will fear no evil, for Thou art with me."

Right here there is a very interesting turn in the Psalm. Up to this point in Psalm 23, David speaks of God in the third person. "The Lord is my shepherd," he says, "I shall not want. *He* maketh me to lie down in green pastures, *He* leadeth me beside the still waters, *He* restoreth my soul. *He* leadeth me in the paths of righteousness for His name's sake." (Psalm 23:1-3) But now in this verse, he suddenly switches to addressing God directly: "I will fear no evil, for *Thou* art with me." (Psalm 23:4) Clearly, David at this point is doing much more than talking *about* God; he is affirming and taking hold of a direct personal connection *with* God. He is experiencing the real presence of God, to lead him through the valley.

The phrase, "Thou art with me," says that we are never alone. The psalm does not promise that we will never be in a valley, nor does it suggest that the valleys of life will be easy; some valleys are very dark and very long and very hard. But the psalm assures us that even in the deepest valleys the Lord is walking alongside us. This message of God's intimate presence comes to its ultimate fulfillment in the New Testament in the birth of Jesus, who is called Emmanuel – *God with us.* (Matthew 1:23)

But what then can be said about the valley itself? The psalm at this point gives further enormous encouragement through a single key word – the word, "through." "Yea, though I walk *through* the valley." The clear message is that we are not stuck in the valley. The Shepherd will lead us through. The Lord our Shepherd will lead us finally through death itself! When we trust in God, we can have confidence that we are moving toward a bright future.

This image of moving through the valley connects with another aspect of shepherding in the Middle East. It is common practice for shepherds to move their flocks during the hot dry summer season to higher elevations, where it is cooler and wetter and the forage is more plentiful. Often the way to get through the hills to higher ground is by traveling up the ravines that cut through the hills. The ravines may appear dangerous and frightening; sheep may be nervous in traversing the difficult ground, but in the process of traveling through these valleys the flock is moving toward better pastures. Often people find that a time of being in a dark valley is a time when they become more closely connected with God and ultimately are able to move spiritually into higher ground.

In the story of David, God did lead him "through the valley" with regard to the rebellion of Absalom. Early on, circumstances looked quite grim for David; but with God's sustenance and help he was able to regroup, and in a climactic battle David's forces finally defeated those of Absalom. David would return to Jerusalem as king.

In the whole struggle with Absalom, a notable additional factor was that David found support not only through God's strengthening and guiding hand, but also through several companions who stood by him. There was David's faithful general Joab, who would provide decisive leadership for David's forces, and there was his good friend and advisor, Hushai. After David had fled from Jerusalem, Hushai planted himself in the capital city and pretended to proclaim allegiance to Absalom. He then gave Absalom bad advice, causing Absalom to delay in his pursuit of David. This proved decisive for David, because it gave him time to recover and finally mount an effective resistance to the rebellion.

When you are in the dark valley, it helps to have friends! Right here is an excellent illustration of the power of the church. When we are journeying through the valley, God gives us companions, connecting us with others in the church, so that we can support and help one another on the way. As Paul said to the church at Thessalonika, "Encourage one another and build each other up." (I Thessalonians 5:11)

In Psalm 23, David is quite clear that the life of faith does not mean that we are spared the dark valleys. Difficult times come – sometimes because of our own mistakes and failings, sometimes because of the actions of others, or sometimes simply because of the vicissitudes of life. Faith does not mean that we are released from difficulty; it means that we can be released from *fear* – as we know and trust in the presence of God. The twenty-third Psalm thus directs us in what we can do when we find ourselves in the valley: look to the Lord our Shepherd, and let the Lord lead us toward a future that finally is glorious and everlasting.

Finding Comfort in Uncomfortable Times

Thy rod and thy staff, they comfort me.
Psalm 23:4b

The one word in this short phrase that leaps out to most people is the word "comfort." People today, of course, enjoy a good deal of material comforts. Yet there is much that brings people discomfort. Health troubles, aches and pains, conflicts in relationships, stresses at work, and the inherent uncertainties of life are all sources of discomfort, and the discomfort becomes amplified as people look to the world at large, and view with dismay all the turmoil and trouble of our nation and world. Such discomfort is an age-old feature of our human condition. When David wrote Psalm 23, he was in the midst of enormous discomfort.

Yet in the psalm he writes of comfort. The Hebrew word translated as "comfort" is the word *nacham* נָחַם, which appears at numerous memorable places in the Old Testament, such as the beginning of Isaiah chapter 40, in words put to music in Handel's *Messiah*: "Comfort ye, comfort ye my people, saith your God." (Isaiah 40:1) The Hebrew *nacham* has the root meaning of drawing a deep breath, or being able to breathe freely. Surely this is one of the deep spiritual needs of every person—in the face of all that assails and troubles us, to be able to breathe free, to be at peace, to find comfort.

But where exactly can people find such comfort? Psalm 23 says that we will find comfort in the Shepherd's rod and staff. Once again, David provides imagery drawn from the Biblical shepherd. The shepherd's staff was the typical shepherd's implement that is commonly depicted in images of Biblical shepherds; it was a long pole, generally with a crook at the end. The Hebrew word for "staff" is מִשְׁעֶנֶת *misheneth*; it comes from a verb meaning "to support"; and indeed the Biblical shepherd would often lean on the staff, using it as a kind of walking stick. But the staff was principally a tool that the shepherd used for the benefit of the sheep. The shepherd would guide sheep with the staff, tapping on the sheep or pressing the lower part of the staff against the sheep to direct them in the right way; and the shepherd would use the staff to rescue sheep that had gotten stuck in brambles or had fallen into a hole. The crook at the top end of the staff was designed to grab under a sheep's leg so as to pull the sheep out of trouble.

But while the staff was ideal for guiding sheep or rescuing sheep, it was not so useful if the shepherd needed to protect the sheep from predators. Here is where the "rod" comes in. When Psalm 23 speaks of a staff and a rod, it uses two completely different Hebrew words. The rod is the Hebrew word שֵׁבֶט *shevet*, which basically means a club. A *shevet* was generally about thirty inches long, with a tapered handle, and a knobbed end. Sometimes bits of metal or stone were embedded into the round end; the shepherd used the rod to clobber any predator that threatened the sheep.

Phillip Keller, who spent time decades ago with shepherds in the Middle East and east Africa, spoke of seeing shepherd boys in the Middle East making these kinds of rods or clubs—and learning to throw them with considerable accuracy. He also spoke of being with some Masai shepherds in Africa who were using these kinds of shepherd's rods; they were moving along with their sheep when at one point they came upon a cobra that was curled, ready to strike. With lightning speed, a young shepherd hammered the snake with his club, putting a quick end to the threat.[vi] The shepherd's rod was an instrument for the defense of the sheep.

The rod also could be used to guide the sheep, much like the staff in that respect; and it was used for the care of the sheep. There was an ancient Hebrew expression—"passing under the rod"—which referred to how shepherds would examine their sheep by bringing them under their rod and using the rod to push back the sheep's wool to look for diseases or parasites or wounds in the sheep.

All of this imagery says something very important about God. Often people think of God as a nebulous and distant figure, who is viewing humanity from afar. But when David in Psalm 23 says that God is like a shepherd, he is saying that God is intimately and actively engaged in our daily life. God is here to help us when we are in trouble, to rescue us when we get ourselves ensnared in difficulty, to defend us in the face of threats, and to guide us in the right way. The rod and staff image tells us that God is a God of power and of compassion, and that God is at work for our benefit. It becomes clear where we can find comfort—when we place ourselves under the care and guidance of the Shepherd.

Our understanding of the imagery in Psalm 23 can also help to illuminate some other Scripture teachings. Consider, for example, Proverbs 13:24—"Those who spare the rod hate their children, but those who love them are diligent to discipline them." From this verse comes the saying, "spare the rod and spoil the child." Often in history this has been understood to mean that children need to be beaten if they are to come out right. But the word "rod" in Proverbs is exactly the same Hebrew word that is used in Psalm 23; and a shepherd would never use the rod to beat the sheep! The rod was an instrument for the care, the protection, the oversight, and the guidance of the sheep. When we understand that, we gain new understanding of the phrase, "spare the rod and spoil the child."

Psalm 23 can also help us to understand some of the teaching of Jesus. Jesus told His disciples that when He departed from this earth, He would send them the Holy Spirit, whom he described as "the Comforter." (John 14:16,26) In essence, the Holy Spirit continues the comforting work of the Good Shepherd. The Holy Spirit is God immediately present with us—here now to guide us, to help us, and to enable us to experience the real comfort of God.

In sum, the Psalm encourages us that we can find genuine comfort—we can "breathe free"—when we trust in the Lord our Shepherd. But here it is very important to recognize that to be *comforted* is not the same thing as to be *comfortable*. Modern society devotes great effort towards trying to be comfortable. Most people in America have comfortable houses and comfortable clothes and comfortable cars. But there are many people who live in very comfortable circumstances who still are not comforted, but who are plagued with all sorts of anxieties and personal turmoil.

If you look at what God does throughout the Bible, you find that God is actually not very much in the business of making people comfortable. Often God seems to be in the opposite business. Moses was comfortable herding some sheep in Midian, but God laid hold of him and sent him to Egypt to rescue the people of Israel from the Pharaoh—a most uncomfortable task! David was comfortable tending to his father's sheep, but God anointed him to be the future king of Israel, and he ended up fighting Goliath and dealing with all sorts of huge challenges. The disciples would have been a lot more comfortable if they had stayed in their fishing boats, but Jesus called them into the very difficult task of being "fishers of people." Following God's call seems to bring people into discomfort. So Paul in his letters speaks of the many discomforts he experienced after he became a missionary for Christ—how he was beaten and imprisoned and shipwrecked on account of his witness. Yet Paul could write, "Just as the sufferings of Christ are abundant for us, so also our comfort is abundant through Christ." (II Cor. 1:5) Though often uncomfortable, Paul and the people of faith before him experienced profound spiritual comfort as they lived in harmony with God and God's purposes, and as they felt God's presence and guidance and help.

It is notable that as Paul and the disciples and David and Moses experienced God's comfort, they did not simply bask in feelings of comfort, but they subsequently became powerful instruments of God's comfort for others. Paul expressed this dynamic in his second letter to the Corinthians, in these words:

"Blessed be the God and Father of our Lord Jesus Christ, the Father of mercies and the God of all comfort, who comforts us in all our tribulation, that we may be able to comfort those who are in any affliction, with the comfort with which we ourselves are comforted by God." (II Cor. 1:3-4) God comforts us "so that we may be able to comfort those who are in any affliction, with the comfort with which we ourselves are comforted by God." Clearly, God is comforting us not so that we can be comfortable, but so that we can finally be instruments of comfort for others.

Now we have the full picture. God is leading us as the Lord's flock not just so that we will have a pleasant stroll but so that we can participate in God's eternal purposes. As we journey with God, we can know, and share, the comfort of the Lord.

God's Abundant Table

Thou preparest a table before me in the presence of mine enemies.
Psalm 23:5a

Many congregations can identify with the image of "preparing a table," because people in churches are often putting on church meals! Sharing a meal is a significant element in many Biblical stories, and of course the image of sharing a meal comes to particular significance in Jesus, who would feed the multitude, who would symbolize heaven with the picture of a banquet, and who would finally represent his own saving sacrifice in the sacramental meal of Communion. In the Bible, sharing a meal is both a feature of many events and an image of great spiritual significance. This can very much be seen in the fifth verse of Psalm 23.

Throughout the first four verses of the psalm, every line is full of shepherd imagery. From the opening phrase–"The Lord is my shepherd"–to the end of verse 4–"thy rod and thy staff, they comfort me"–the psalm consistently pictures God as a shepherd. But now in verse 5 the imagery shifts to the image of a gracious host: "Thou preparest a table before me in the presence of mine enemies, thou anointest my head with oil, my cup runneth over." Some interpreters have tried to insist that all this could still refer to the life of a Biblical shepherd with the sheep. The "table in the presence of enemies" would be a lush pasture with wolves all around.

The "anointing with oil" would refer to putting bug repellant on sheep's heads; and the "cup running over" would refer to a water hole overflowing with water. Surely this stretches things a bit! It makes much more sense to recognize that David at this point in Psalm 23 is simply transitioning images from that of a shepherd to that of a host. German scholars like to say that Psalm 23 refers to God as "Hirt und Wirt"–shepherd and host–and while it is not possible to get the same clever word play in English, it is easy to see that these two images fit naturally together, because in Biblical times, shepherds often did serve in the role of host. In the ancient near east, one of the strongest traditions among shepherds was a tradition of hospitality. If a weary traveler showed up at a shepherd's tent, the honorable shepherd would provide gracious hospitality, giving the traveler food and drink and refreshment. A prime example of this can be found in the story of Abraham, who while managing his flocks was approached by three mysterious travelers. Genesis reports that "When Abraham saw them, he ran from the tent entrance to meet them, bowed to the ground, and said, 'Do not pass by, but let a little water be brought to wash your feet, and rest yourselves under the tree. Let me bring bread, that you may refresh yourselves.'" (Genesis 18:3–5) When they stayed, he not only brought bread, but prepared a full meal for them with veal and curds and milk. He did not yet know that they were actually emissaries of God. But Abraham, an upright and righteous shepherd, was a gracious host.

So is it clear what is happening in Psalm 23. Having created the image of God as a good shepherd, the psalm now continues with the image of God as a gracious host. The message is that we can find welcome and sustenance in God. When we are weary and weak, God receives us with grace, and would set before us an abundant table. God invites us into God's presence, to refresh our spirits and bestow blessing upon us.

At this juncture, one can note a connection between Psalm 23 and multiple points in the Bible where God acted decisively to provide abundant nourishment for weary travelers. When the people of Israel were wandering through the wilderness, God provided manna for them to eat and sources of water; and during the ministry of Jesus, when a large crowd had followed Jesus to a remote place, Jesus provided the miraculous feeding of the 5,000. In these accounts, God provided literal food; but this was also symbolic for how God would provide spiritually all that we need.

"Thou preparest a table before me" is thus a powerful statement of the providence of God. But then the verse goes on, with a phrase that may seem odd: "Thou preparest a table before me *in the presence of mine enemies.*" This creates the rather unusual picture of someone enjoying a banquet while enemies are nearby. It is this verse that provides a primary reason for why Biblical scholars place the writing of Psalm 23 during the rebellion of Absalom, because it was in the midst of that rebellion, when David had taken refuge in the town of Mahanaim, that he had precisely this experience of having a table prepared before him in the presence of his enemies.

The story of Absalom is a story that might seem ready-made for a TV series or a movie today; because it is a story loaded with sordid elements. Absalom was one of David's many sons, born to one of David's many wives. Absalom was the son of David's wife Maacah, and through Maacah David also had a daughter, Tamar. Absalom had an older brother named Amnon, who was born to David's wife, Ahinoam. So Absalom and Amnon were half-brothers, while Absalom and Tamar were full brother and sister.

Amnon lusted after Tamar. He got her into a room and raped her. David, while a great king, was not a very attentive father; and he did nothing to discipline Amnon. Absalom thereupon took vengeance into his own hands, and he murdered Amnon. David did nothing to discipline Absalom either but allowed him to live freely. Absalom, however, came to realize that David was not going to let him become the eventual king; so he decided to seize the throne for himself. In II Samuel 15, there is an account of how Absalom gathered people around him who were disgruntled with King David; and he told them that if he, Absalom, were king, they would get what they wanted. That a politician would promise to give people what they want is a familiar scenario to us! Absalom thus built up a following, and finally he launched the full-scale rebellion described in the previous chapters.

As David, along with a small band of compatriots, fled from Jerusalem, he entered into a journey that was not only long but miserable. David was full of grief and anxiety, and he was even tormented along the way. There was a man named Shimei, who was of the family of Saul, who resented David and who now took this opportunity to heap insult onto injury. The book of II Samuel in chapter 16 reports that "Shimei approached and cursed continually, and threw stones at David, and at David's servants, and shouted, 'Begone, you worthless fellow! The Lord has avenged all the blood of the household of Saul, in whose place you have reigned, and the Lord has now given the kingdom into the hand of your son Absalom! See, your ruin is upon you.'" (II Samuel 16:5–8) Shimei did all this from a distance, from the far side of a ravine. David's bodyguards wanted to run over and cut Shimei to pieces. But David told them to let him go.

By the time David arrived at the town of Mahanaim where he would find shelter, he was physically and emotionally spent. Then II Samuel reports, "When David came to Mahanaim, Shobi son of Nahash from Rabbah of the Ammonites, and Machir the son of Ammiel from Lodebar, and Barzillai the Gileadite brought beds, basins, and earthen vessels, wheat, barley, meal, parched grain, beans and lentils, honey and curds and sheep and cheese from the herd, for David and the people with him to eat; for they said, 'The people are hungry and weary and thirsty in the wilderness.'" (II Samuel 17:27-29)

At one of the lowest points in David's life, in the midst of betrayal and threat, with his enemies pressing upon him, God provided an abundant table. David's experience of this gracious banquet in the face of pending attack provided the clear occasion for his verse in the psalm: "Thou preparest a table before me in the presence of mine enemies." Refreshed and greatly encouraged, David subsequently began to build up support, using Mahanaim as a base. The banquet had provided a crucial spiritual as well as physical uplift. A downcast David had received caring support and strengthening help.

It is notable how that help arrived—via a group of caring people. David's story thus illustrates how God's people today are to be instruments of God's care and support for others. In this respect, Shobi and Machir and Barzillai form a striking picture of what the church is to be—a community organized to extend help to those in need. It is interesting that the help they provided was in the form of food, since this is something churches continue to often do! One of the prominent ministries for many churches today is the work of providing an "abundant table" for the poor in the community, through meal programs and food pantries.

There is another very interesting feature of David's story in the identities of the people in that caring community. The group bringing food to David's entourage included Shobi, who was not a Hebrew but an Ammonite, a member of a neighboring kingdom. The group also included Barzillai, who is identified as a Gileadite, meaning that he was living amongst that Hebrew clan; but Barzillai is not a Hebrew name. It is an Aramaean name, which leads many Biblical scholars to conclude that he also was a non-Israelite, an Aramaean who as a foreigner had joined the Israelite community. Two of the three key people who helped David were thus not native Israelites. David's entourage itself also included non-Israelites. In the account of David's flight from Jerusalem, there is a story about six hundred Gittites—a non-Israelite group from Philistia—who had recently immigrated and who chose to stick with David as he fled from Jerusalem toward Mahanaim. II Samuel 15 reports that "David said to Ittai the Gittite, 'Why are you also coming with us? Go back, for you are a foreigner, and also an exile from your home. You came only yesterday, and shall I make you now wander about with us? Go back, and may the Lord show steadfast love and faithfulness to you.'" (II Samuel 15:19–20) David kindly urged Ittai, the leader of the Gittite group, that they did not need to get caught up in David's troubles. "But Ittai," the Scripture reports, "answered the king, 'As the Lord lives, wherever my lord the king may be, whether for death or for life, there also your servant will be.'" (II Samuel 15:21) The remarkable picture here is that while David's own son was betraying him, Ittai, a foreigner, pledged unshakable allegiance to David; and while David's son wanted to take everything away from David, two other foreigners, Barzillai and Shobi, along with the Israelite Machir, stepped forward to give David generous and critical help. This again provides a foretaste of what the church is to be—a community of every race and nation that joins together in a common commitment to God and God's purposes.

David thus received crucial support from this network of friends; and David in gratitude would later offer to reward them each for their loyalty. At the same time, David was also clear that the most important help that he was receiving was the help of God; for it was God who was inspiring people to help David and who was powerfully at work in all that was unfolding. Thus in Psalm 23

David would not finally write, "My friends prepare a table before me in the presence of mine enemies," but rather he would address God: "Thou preparest a table before me in the presence of mine enemies." David knew that God was the ultimate source of all blessing; and he knew further that his greatest need, by far, was not for any earthly banquet of good things but for the grace and strength and promise of God.

Jesus carried this theme forward when he referred to the food that God provided in Old Testament days and said, "Your ancestors ate the manna in the wilderness... and they died. I am the living bread which comes down from heaven, that a person may partake of it and not die." (John 6:49,51) Once again, food in the Scripture provides a clear spiritual image. As much as we may value the many material blessings that we receive from God, our deepest need is spiritual – the need for a life-giving connection with God. Jesus is that "living bread" – the gift of God that nourishes the soul. This is profoundly symbolized whenever believers partake in the sacrament of Communion, as it provides an ongoing way for believers to experience what David did: that no matter what "enemies" we may face in life, the Lord provides a table that is abundant and everlasting.

The Anointing

Thou anointest my head with oil
                                                           Psalm 23:5b

For modern readers, the phrase, "thou anointest my head with oil," is perhaps the most obscure phrase in all of Psalm 23. We don't anoint one another with oil, and most people when they hear these words are not at all sure what to make of them. Ancient people, however, would have known exactly what David was talking about, because anointing with oil was a very common ancient practice. In the ancient near east, if a host wanted to be especially gracious to a guest, the host would place a perfumed oil–generally olive oil with natural fragrances mixed in–onto the guest's head. People at the time felt that having copious oil poured over your head was something just wonderful. You can find an expression of this, for example, in Psalm 133, which says, "How good and pleasant it is when kindred live together in unity; it is like precious oil on the head, running down the beard… running over the collar." (Psalm 133:1-2)

This sounds like a mess! You read a passage like this and might start thinking about taking a shower. But in Biblical times, it was precisely because people did not so often take a shower, or a bath, that they loved oil like this. Rich people would use perfumed oil in the morning to freshen up; and if a traveler came into a house or a tent after a journey–dusty, wind-blown, sweaty, one's long hair a tangle – having a nicely scented oil applied to one's head was experienced as especially refreshing. It was also experienced as especially gracious, since perfumed oil was expensive, and hosts did not do this for everybody. To be anointed with oil was to be honored.

In the gospels, there are two significant moments when Jesus was anointed with oil. Once when Jesus was in the home of a Pharisee having dinner, a woman of poor reputation entered the house, and she began to anoint Jesus' feet.[vii] People would normally wash their feet, but they would not waste oil on their feet; the fact that the woman poured oil on Jesus' feet was an expression of her humility and an expression of the extravagance of her gift. The Pharisee thought the whole thing to be unseemly; but Jesus said to him, "You did not anoint my head with oil" – the Pharisee was not very gracious toward Jesus – "but she has anointed my feet." (Luke 7:46) The woman had exemplified a humble graciousness. In another account, shortly before the crucifixion, a woman came up to Jesus and anointed his head with expensive oil.[viii] Some of the disciples complained that the oil could have been sold for a good price; but Jesus said that the woman had anointed his body for burial – a sign of his impending self-sacrifice – and he affirmed the woman. In each case, the anointing with oil was recognized by Jesus as a beautiful expression of extravagant love and honor, and in each case Jesus in return blessed the woman with grace.

So when David said of God, "You anoint my head with oil," he was saying is that God is like a gracious host who extravagantly welcomes us with honor and love and blessing. But what happens if we are sinners, unworthy of God's honor? How does God view us if our life has been far from spiritual perfection? Does God look at us as the Pharisee might, and decide to withhold blessing, or as those grumbling disciples might, and decide that divine blessing is better spent elsewhere? When David, himself guilty of very serious sin in his past, said of God, "Thou anointest my head with oil," he was saying that God meets even the worst sinner with abundant grace. God meets us in our weakness and imperfection and need, and pours out mercy and promise upon us. This is something that we can each experience today through Jesus Christ, as God is at work to freely and extravagantly bestow God's love upon us.

But God does not bless us so abundantly in order that we now might sit back and simply think how nice it is to be blessed by God. There is another key aspect to God's anointing. In Biblical times, there were actually two kinds of anointing. One kind was the anointing of a guest by a host, which was an expression of gracious favor. But if you look at the story of David and ask, "Where specifically do we have a story of David being anointed?" you come upon the other kind of anointing. This is described in the book of I Samuel, when the prophet Samuel anointed the young David to be the future king of Israel. I Samuel 16 reports, "Then Samuel took the horn of oil, and anointed David in the presence of his brothers, and the spirit of the Lord came mightily upon David from that day forward." (I Samuel 16:13) This anointing was a consecration of a person for service. Kings and priests were all typically anointed in this way. Here the pouring of the oil was a symbol of God's Spirit being poured into a person. David as he was anointed by Samuel was empowered by God to serve the people of Israel and to eventually become their king.

The ultimate Biblical example of someone being anointed for service is Jesus. The word "Messiah" means "the anointed one," and the New Testament speaks of Jesus as having been anointed by God, as in Acts 10:38, where Peter declares, "God anointed Jesus of Nazareth with the Holy Spirit and with power, and He went about doing good and healing."

To be anointed in this sense is to be empowered by God's Spirit to serve God in the world. The New Testament declares that God through Christ is at work now to anoint each of us in this way. As it is said in I John, "You have been anointed by the Holy One." (I John 2:20). God's anointing would thus not only bless us, but would move us to join with God in carrying God's blessing to others. This connects directly with the next image in the psalm – that of the overflowing cup.

The Overflowing Cup

My cup runneth over
        Psalm 23:5c

People often talk about whether the cup is half full or half empty. David says, "My cup runneth over." Some people might say, "Sure, his cup runs over. He's king! He's powerful, successful, and rich." But the situation changes when we realize that David wrote the psalm during one of the most horrendous periods in his life, when his own son Absalom had betrayed him and was coming after him with an army. David at this juncture might very well have said, "Lord, my cup is getting rather empty!" But instead he proclaimed, "My cup runneth over."

How could David say that? It is because he measured his life not in terms of earthly fortune but in terms of God's goodness. He knew that God was with him, with overflowing grace and blessing and promise; and by that measure, even in a time of great trouble, he could say "My cup runneth over." The apostle Paul made similar statements. In numerous places in his letters he referred to the many sufferings he endured on his missionary journeys, yet he always praised God for the abundance of God's goodness and what he called "God's surpassing grace." (II Corinthians 9:14)

We deal with times in life when it may seem that our cup is getting quite empty. In such times the pleasant imagery of Psalm 23 may appear irrelevant. Who can relate to a picture of still waters when the waters in your own life are frighteningly rough, or the picture of an overflowing cup when yours seems to have nothing? This is why it is so important to remember the circumstances in which David actually wrote the psalm. The images of peace and abundance in the psalm do not depict the outward circumstances in his life; they speak to the condition of his soul. The psalm tells us that, even in rough times, our cup can overflow with strength and peace when we put our trust in God.

Still further, it is notable that the image is not simply of a cup that is full but a cup that "runneth over." The Hebrew word here, רְוָיָה *revayah*, indicates a superabundance. God provides more than enough, something that David literally experienced in the abundant table that was set by his supporters. But what finally does one do with the superabundance of God's blessing? The consistent Biblical message is that our cup "runneth over" in order that God's goodness might flow from us to others! And as God's grace overflows from us, it overflows from other people's lives yet further. Paul described this dynamic in II Corinthians, at a time when he was taking a charitable collection, when he said, "The rendering of generous service not only supplies the needs of the saints but also overflows in many thanksgivings to God." (II Corinthians 9:12)

In the twenty-third Psalm, David is clear that God is the source of wondrous blessing—it is God who provides an abundant table, who anoints us, and who fills our cup to overflowing—and he is clear that the purpose of this blessing is so that we ourselves can carry out God's good works in the world. But if David is a picture of a person whose life finally is directed toward God and inspired by God, one can see the opposite and sharply contrasting picture in the figure of Absalom.

David, as noted in the previous chapter, was anointed by God, who chose him through the prophet Samuel, and David knew that his anointing was a commission to serve God. Absalom, in contrast, anointed himself, setting up his own coronation in the city of Hebron, and he saw the anointing as his pathway to personal grandeur. His aim was to usurp the throne, not because he sincerely sought a better government, but because he wanted wealth and glory. Absalom is a picture of human pride and the quest for power—the way that many people try to advance themselves in this world with no thought for God, or what is truly right.

It should be no surprise that Absalom was especially known for his vanity. The Bible notes that this was particularly expressed in the attention he gave to his long flowing hair. The book of II Samuel reports, "Now in all Israel, there was no one to be praised for his beauty as Absalom; from the sole of his foot to the crown of his head there was no blemish in him. And when he cut the hair of his head (for at the end of every year he used to cut it, when it was heavy on him), he weighed the hair of his head, two hundred shekels by the king's weight [that is, about five pounds]." (II Samuel 15:25-26) Absalom could have been the inspiration for Gaston in Disney's Beauty and the Beast! He thought a whole lot of himself, he managed to impress other people, and he was all about elevating himself; but he ultimately would become an illustration of Jesus' saying that those who exalt themselves will be humbled.

The rebellion led by Absalom came finally to a climax in the forest of Ephraim, where a great battle unfolded between the forces of Absalom and those of David. David's forces, trusting in God, prevailed over those of Absalom; and Absalom fled, riding on a mule. But the book of II Samuel reports that as he sped through the forest, as fast as one can go on a mule, his head got caught in the branches of an oak.[ix] The implication is that his long hair, that he so treasured, got so entangled in the low branches that he was left dangling by his hair as the mule ran on. In that most inglorious position he was found by David's hard-nosed general Joab, who ran three spears through him, bringing Absalom's quest for glory to a most ignominious end. Absalom finally is a picture of the self-focused life, which ends in emptiness.

The figures of David and Absalom thus present two radically contrasting approaches to living. Those who follow in the way of Absalom are always obsessed with what they think they lack, and they spend their lives grasping, sometimes shoving others out of the way in the process; but they find that their cup never gets full. Those who gain the spiritual insight of the twenty-third Psalm look to God and find, along with David, the anointing of God's grace and the cup that truly overflows.

Surely Goodness and Mercy Shall Follow Me

Surely goodness and mercy shall follow me all the days of my life

Psalm 23:6a

Two key words jump out immediately in verse six. The first is "goodness," a word that might seem to people to be milquetoast sort of term. But in the present day and age, there is a real longing for goodness. Would you not wish to look at the news one day and find that the top stories are all about goodness? Too often, in the continual human quest after wealth and power, goodness has been underrated. But clearly what the world desperately needs today is an increase in goodness!

The Bible says that goodness has its origin in God. The Psalms declare that "God is good" (Psalms 100:5, 107:1), and when God creates the universe, Genesis declares that "God saw that it [the creation] was good" (Genesis 1:4,10,12,18,21,25). The Hebrew word being translated as "good" in these passages and in Psalm 23 is the word טוֹב *tov*—which has the same basic meaning as our English word for goodness. It indicates that which is positive, beneficial, and morally upright. The clear message is that if the world is not good, it is because people have turned from God and departed from God's design for human living. If we want a life that is authentically good, we need to look to God.

The second key word in Psalm 23 verse 6 is the word "mercy." Here the English term "mercy" is partly getting at the underlying Hebrew word, but there is more to it. The original Hebrew word at this point is the word חֶסֶד *chesed*—which is one of the most important words in the entire Bible. It means "steadfast love"—love that never quits, love that never gives up even in the face of disappointment, love that is poured out even if it is undeserved. *Chesed* includes mercy and forgiveness and unbounded compassion. It is the number one word used in the Old Testament to describe the nature and character of God. Steadfast love is the sort of love that God continually shows toward the people of Israel, and the kind of love that God ultimately shows toward the whole world in Jesus. Even as human beings so often fall short of God's goodness, God does not give up on us, but reaches to us with mercy and compassion .

Tov and *chesed*—goodness and steadfast love—are very often used together in the Bible. Several Psalms, for example, contain the line, "O give thanks to the Lord, for He is good, for His steadfast love endures forever." (Psalm 100:5, 106:1, 107:1, 118:1) This coupling of these two words is highly significant. In Jesus' day, there were some people who thought of themselves as good—especially the Pharisees—because they held to a certain idea of righteous living; but they often did not treat other people in a loving fashion. Jesus challenged them at precisely that point, because according to Jesus, the good action is the loving action. This principle relates very much to our own time.

At the end of October in 2018, the top religion news was the decision by the Pakistan Supreme Court to acquit Asia Bibi, who, in 2010, had been condemned to death for supposedly insulting the prophet Mohammed. As a Christian, Asia was part of the tiny Christian minority in Pakistan which is often cruelly oppressed. She was working in fields one day along with some Muslim women, when the Muslim women refused to drink water from a container because Asia, a Christian, had touched it and thereby, in their view, fouled the water. There ensued some words between the women. The Muslim women pressed upon Asia that she should convert to Islam; Asia resisted. A few days later, a couple of the Muslim women accused Asia of blasphemy. Pakistan's blasphemy law states that any derogatory remarks toward Mohammed must result in a mandatory death penalty. Asia was found guilty and sentenced to death, but she appealed the ruling. Through the years, prominent people tried to intercede on her behalf. In 2011, both the provincial governor, Salman Taseer, and the minister of minorities, Shahbaz Bhatti, spoke out in Asia's defense and criticized the use of the blasphemy law. They were both assassinated. Pope Benedict got involved; so did Pope Francis. Appellate courts continued to uphold the death sentence, until the Supreme Court reversed the sentence, setting the stage for Asia to go free. Many people in Pakistan, including many Muslims, applauded the ruling, longing for a more tolerant society. But immediately following the ruling, there were large marches of angry religious extremists, calling for Asia to hanged, and also calling for the murders of all the judges on the court. Asia's lawyer fled Pakistan, fearing that otherwise he would surely be killed. Asia began to seek asylum outside of Pakistan; but her future remained gravely in doubt, as crowds chanted vehemently against her, holding signs that read, "Hang Asia."

The people in those hate-filled crowds would want to think of themselves as the "good people" in that society. But the Biblical Word makes clear—the good people are those who are also merciful.

Jesus' critique of the Pharisees—that those who imagine themselves to be pious and righteous are not good if they are also hateful—thus applies afresh to our own day.

Of course, Jesus is also speaking to each one of us. We are called to express authentic goodness *by showing compassion and mercy* – and not just toward our friends and family members, but toward people who are different from us and who are very imperfect, which is the kind of love God shows.

One might conclude at this point that everyone should simply aspire to be more good and loving. That is fine; but our human problem is that we often fall short even of our own best aspirations. How then can we arrive at goodness and mercy? Here David says something quite striking in the twenty-third Psalm when he continues and says, "Surely goodness and mercy shall *follow* me." The Hebrew word translated "follow" is the verb, רָדַף *radaph*, which actually means "to pursue," and it especially means to pursue relentlessly. In the Bible, the word is sometimes used to describe armies doggedly pursuing their opponents, or a person will speak of being pursued by enemies. David might have thought about how he was being pursued by Absalom and his rebel army. We might think of how problems are bearing down on us. But in Psalm 23, David says, "I am being pursued by goodness and mercy." What an image – you are being chased, and chased relentlessly, by goodness and mercy!

This is a complete reversal of our usual way of thinking. Typically we might think of how trouble is chasing us; or if we think of goodness and mercy, we think of how we need to pursue – we need to strive after – goodness and mercy. But Psalm 23 says that God's goodness and steadfast love are pursuing us! In fact, this is what the Biblical story again and again portrays. God in steadfast love relentlessly pursues the people of Israel, even as they often wander away from God. God keeps after them to show them goodness and compassion. And God does this finally for the whole world in Jesus Christ. We are sinners, often failing to achieve goodness or live in love;

we are like lost sheep wandering in a land of trouble. But in Christ, God pursues us; the Shepherd comes after us, to pour mercy upon us, to bless us with goodness, and to guide us in steadfast love. If we wish, therefore, to live a life of goodness and mercy, it is not something we must accomplish on our own. We can know God's love and be brought more and more into goodness and mercy as we open ourselves to how God is reaching to us with grace. The idea that God relentlessly pursues humanity with goodness and mercy brings real hope as well for the whole world, for it means that no matter how bad things may get or how askew humanity may be, God is not giving up on us.

All this relates to the last part of the phrase, where it says that goodness and mercy will follow me *all the days of my life*. Here is a powerful declaration that God's goodness and love never end. Even when we have times of serious trouble, such as David was certainly having during the rebellion of Absalom, we can know that God is reaching to us with goodness and help. Even when we stumble badly in life, we can know that God is at hand to lift us up. Even when we encounter death, we can have confidence that God's goodness and mercy will be with us. This is a promise that comes then to its ultimate fruition in the final statement of the Psalm: "And I will dwell in the house of the Lord forever."

I Will Dwell in the House of the Lord Forever

... and I will dwell in the house of the Lord forever.
Psalm 23:6b

It has been suggested that part of the appeal of Psalm 23 for many people might be that it seems to be all promise and no demands. The psalm speaks of God leading us beside still waters, filling our cup to overflowing, bestowing upon us goodness and mercy; and the psalm, on the face of it, does not appear to ask anything of us in return. But in fact something *is* required of us, and this becomes especially evident in the final phrase.

"I will dwell in the house of the Lord," says David. When David spoke of the house of the Lord, he surely had in mind, on one level, the tabernacle in Jerusalem, the central place of worship, which was thought of as God's house. In David's day, the tabernacle was still a temporary structure; it would be replaced with a permanent temple by his son Solomon. But whatever its form, the "house of the Lord" was that place where people came together to worship God. Today people rightfully think in the same way of a church building as God's house.

But to dwell in God's house meant more than simply to enter a particular building. At the center of the tabernacle and later the temple in Jerusalem was the ark of the covenant, the gold-covered box that held the ten commandments and that was understood to symbolize the presence of God among the people. When people came into God's house, they had a feeling that they were drawing near to the presence of God. To dwell in God's house meant, above all, to abide with God. It meant to live in God's presence in an attitude of faith and worship.

This idea of God's house comes forth again at later points in the Bible. In Psalm 84, which was written many years after David by a group called the sons of Korah, there are the words, "How lovely is your dwelling place, O Lord of hosts. Happy are those who live in your house, ever singing your praise." (Psalm 84:1,4) Psalm 84 declares that genuine happiness is to be found by entering into God's house–joining in a fellowship with God in which our hearts are lifted to God in praise.

Of course, entering into God's house could just mean a very infrequent visit with God, so David elaborates on the image when he says, "I will dwell in the house of the Lord–forever." The original Hebrew phrase here, translated in the King James Version as "forever," is לְאֹרֶךְ יָמִים (l'orek yamim), which actually means "for the length of days."[x] The essential meaning of the verse is, "I will dwell in the house of the Lord all my days." What David is saying here is that he will dwell in God's house continually. This meant literally that he would worship regularly in the tabernacle, and furthermore it was a spiritual commitment to live every day in fellowship with God. This idea of dwelling daily with God relates to the central concept in the psalm that the Lord is our shepherd. It does the sheep little good if they only live some days in the presence of the shepherd and others not; because if the sheep are not in the presence of the shepherd, they are lost and exposed to wolves. One needs the Shepherd each day. This also relates to the image of God as host, which comes forth in the middle of the psalm, whereby God invites us into God's presence and sets before us an abundant table. If we are to share in God's abundance, we need to enter in and abide in a connection with God. So

I Will Dwell in the House of the Lord Forever

the psalm, having affirmed God's graciousness throughout, concludes with a critical response on our part. We are called to make a commitment to God—to put our faith in God and live daily in a relationship with God.

When people hear Psalm 23 today, they often hear a translation such as the King James Version in which the last line is translated, "I will dwell in the house of the Lord forever," and they think that "forever" is referring to eternal life in heaven. So the psalm seems to them to be saying, "I will dwell in the house of the Lord after I die." But David is not talking about dwelling in God's house after you die. He is talking about dwelling in God's house now. In fact, why would we even think about dwelling in God's house for eternity if we are not already dwelling in God's house today?

So is David thinking about heaven at all? It is important to remember that David lived a thousand years before the resurrection. No one had promised him eternal life; no one had won for him eternal life. In his day, the Israelites as whole actually did not believe in life after death, because God as yet had revealed no such thing. It was only later in the Old Testament that prophets began to catch a glimpse of what God would do in Jesus. So when David concludes Psalm 23 with the phrase לְאֹרֶךְ יָמִים (l'orek yamim), "all my days," he was thinking of all his days on earth. This is why ancient translators, when they were translating the original Hebrew into ancient Greek or Latin, always translated it with the simple meaning of "all my days"[xi]; and the same sort of meaning is found in many modern English translations, such as the New Revised Standard Version, which concludes Psalm 23 with, "I shall dwell in the house of the Lord my whole life long."

So how did the King James Version, and some other modern versions, end up translating the close of Psalm 23 as "I will dwell in the house of the Lord forever"? They did so by reading Psalm 23 in the light of the New Testament. The image of dwelling in God's house was taken up by Jesus, and he used that image to talk about an eternal home that God would create for us. In John chapter 14, where there is an extended discussion of eternal life, Jesus said, "In my Father's house there are many rooms... I go to prepare a place for you." (John 14:2) Jesus was saying that there is an everlasting house of God, and there is a place for you in it. You *can* dwell in God's house forever – by taking hold of the gift of eternal life that is now offered to each of us through Jesus Christ.

Psalm 23 literally says, "I will dwell in the house of the Lord all my days, or as long as I live." So how long is that? In the light of Jesus, it can be forever. The King James translators may have gotten a little free in their translation, but in the light of the gospel, they were absolutely correct to say, "I will dwell in the house of the Lord forever."

What is important to remember is that "forever" begins today! Many people in our society have the odd idea that you don't need to pay much attention to God now; living with God is something you do after you die. But the Biblical picture puts the accent on living with God in the here and now. In Psalm 23, there is the picture throughout the psalm of being guided and blessed by the presence of the Lord, and in Psalm 84, with its picture of God's house, there is an idea of life as a journey of the spirit towards "Zion." Zion in the Old Testament was the hill in Jerusalem upon which the temple or God's house was built; so Psalm 84 pictures life as a journey toward the greater experience of the presence of God. The psalm put it this way: "Happy are those whose strength is in You, in whose heart are the highways to Zion. As they go through the bitter valley they make it a place of springs. They go from strength to strength; they will see God in Zion." (Psalm 84:5-7) The message is that we don't wait until death to be with God. We live and grow today in fellowship with God, and in that journey even the bitter valleys in life can become abundant places and times of growing in strength, because we are in connection with God.

So we dwell in God's house today. But the very image of dwelling in a house with many rooms has another obvious feature – it is not a private enterprise but a matter of joining with other people, who likewise are living in faith. The same idea comes forth in Psalm 23 in the image of the flock of sheep who are living together under the shepherd. Today the popular religious preference is not for such community but rather for private religion. Spirituality is popular; the church is not. Many people like to bash the church – pointing out everything that is wrong with "institutional religion" and everything that is flawed about churches. The fact is, of course, that churches are made up of fallible human beings, and it is inevitable that churches will do things that fall short of perfection or that things will happen in churches that bring us frustration. So it may seem much more comfortable to retreat into private spirituality. But here is another point where Psalm 23 challenges us, for it says that God our Shepherd is calling us into a connection with all those other sheep. This may be tough some days. Those other sheep are going to have some different opinions about things. They might vote differently. Those other sheep are going to do things at times that irritate us. It is impossible to live in community with others without sometimes being disappointed or hurt. So we may begin to say to ourselves, "Forget about God's house. I want my own house." But the testimony of Psalm 23 is clear, as it says: "I will dwell in the house of the Lord." We are invited into God's house which includes all God's people, joining together in the worship of God and in service for God. It is in fact a good thing that the church is full of all sorts of flawed people; because otherwise, how would I get in? The wonderful news is that in spite of our flaws God welcomes all of us into God's house; and it is in community with God and with one another that the grace of God begins to take concrete shape–it takes the shape of forgiving one another and accepting each other; it takes the shape of young people that we help to mentor, or people for whom we pray, or missions to which we respond along with the whole church. Dwelling in God's house is not simply a vague distant idea of an afterlife; it is a living connection with God and God's people in which we share in grace together right now.

At the same time, we take hold of the sure gospel promise that God's house will stand forever. Those who depart from this world do not in fact depart from God's house, but continue to share in a fellowship with God and all the saints in a glorious life everlasting.

It is significant to note that the name of God, the word *Lord*, appears twice, and just twice, in Psalm 23. It appears at the very beginning–"The Lord is my shepherd"–and it appears at the very end–"I will dwell in the house of the Lord forever." The word *Lord* brackets the psalm. This is a way of saying that God is at the beginning, and God is at the end. God brings us into life, God guides us through life as our Shepherd, and God holds our future. When we place our faith in the Lord, we can have confidence that we will not only be upheld in God's presence throughout life here but that indeed "we will dwell in the house of the Lord forever."

Notes

Chapter 2
i.   Hammurabi stele, 35, 18th century BC.

Chapter 4
ii.   Phillip Keller, *A Shepherd Looks at Psalm 23* (Zondervan, 1970), p. 25.

iii.   *Ibid.*, p. 29.

Chapter 6
iv.   See Haddon W. Robinson, *Trusting the Shepherd* (Discovery House Publishers, 1968), p. 51.

Chapter 8
v.   To say that "churches are the source of the great majority of charitable giving" is to recognize that giving arises not only through church channels but that people who are active in churches are particularly motivated to give through other channels as well. The strength of religiously inspired giving has been well documented. Moreover, churches operate in a fashion such that a great deal of giving occurs beyond even what is counted in statistics, as churches regularly take collections of food or clothing, and inspire the giving of enormous amounts of hours of service to the community.

Chapter 10
vi.   Keller, *op cit.*

Chapter 12
vii. "A woman in the city, who was a sinner, having learned that he was eating in the Pharisee's house, brought an alabaster jar of ointment... and

began anointing Jesus' feet with the ointment." Luke 7:38–39

viii. "A woman came to him with an alabaster jar of very costly ointment, and she poured it on Jesus' head as he sat at the table. But when the disciples saw it, they were angry and said, 'Why this waste? For this ointment could have been sold for a large sum.'" Matthew 26:7–9

Chapter 13

ix. "For Absalom was riding on his mule, and the mule went under the thick branches of a great oak. And his head caught fast in the oak, so he was left hanging between heaven and earth, while the mule that was under him kept going." II Samuel 18:9

Chapter 15

x. There is a different Hebrew phrase, לְעוֹלָם *l'olam*, which means "forever."

xi. The Latin Vulgate, for example, from the fourth century AD, renders the ending of the psalm as "et habitabo in domo Domini in longitudine dierum" — "and I will dwell in the house of the Lord unto the length of days."

www.ingramcontent.com/pod-product-compliance
Lightning Source LLC
Chambersburg PA
CBHW020950090426
42736CB00010B/1347